CLASSIC MANDALAS

CLASSIC MANDALAS

74 Designs from the World's Traditions to Color and Meditate

Sterling Publishing Co., Inc.
New York

Library of Congress-in-Publication Data Available

10   9   8   7   6   5   4   3   2   1

Published in 2002 by Sterling Publishing Co., Inc.
387 Park Avenue South, New York, NY 10016
Originally published in Germany under the title *Mandala-Welten*
Malback: 74 Mandalas aus vielen Kulturbereichen zum
Ausmalen und Meditieren by Schirner Verlag
Landwehrstr. 7a, Darmstadt, D-64293
© 1998 by Schirner Verlag
English translation © 2002 by Sterling Publishing Co., Inc.
Translated from the German to English by Nicole Franke and Daniel Shea
Distributed in Canada by Sterling Publishing
c/o Canadian Manda Group, One Atlantic Avenue, Suite 105
Toronto, Ontario, M6K 3E7, Canada
Distributed in Australia by Capricorn Link (Australia) Pty Ltd.
P.O. Box 704, Windsor, NSW 2756, Australia

Printed in China
All rights reserved

Sterling ISBN 1-4027-0037-7

Contents

Introduction .1

Mandalas .3

What Colors Represent 151

Index 153

INTRODUCTION

The theory of holism states that everything in the universe is related and linked together. If one organism is disturbed, for example, all others are affected in some way or another. In order to find ourselves and become "one" again, we need a holistic method of treatment which demands silence, meditation, and guidance. Mandalas offer guidance because they force us to examine our emotions, fears, thoughts, and feelings by pushing our unconscious to our conscious, connecting them into one collective consciousness. *Classic Mandalas: 74 Designs from the World's Traditions to Color and Meditate* has specifically been designed for the needs of adults. From Africa to Polynesia, from the Australian Aborigines to the Native Americans, from Buddhism to Christianity, these seventy-four mandalas represent many different cultures and religions so that you, the colorer, may be able to find yourself and recognize what it is that *you* need in order to become one again in this holistic universe.

ABOUT THE ILLUSTRATOR

Early in life, Heike Owusu gained a spiritual world-view that, at first, found little sympathy from her family and social circles. When a serious illness threatened her life, she overcame it with the help of relaxation and a personally developed self-healing method. Her marriage to a Ghanaian man only intensified her already great interest in the wisdom of primitive peoples and their mythologies. All of this released her artistic creativity, and so today she expresses her insights through the shapes of cosmic pictures, illustrations, and literary work.

MAGICAL ENERGY MANDALA

This mandala signifies the fusion of the inner and outer worlds into one cosmic Unity. The base, the ninth key shaped into three hearts by three snakes, stands as a symbol of singularity and feminine principles. To the right and left is the sign of the double axe, which represents the moon's waxing and waning, thus also life and death.

PEACOCK MANDALA

The peacock's tail, with one hundred eyes, is a symbol of vigilance and immortality.

SPHINX MANDALA

This mandala symbolizes the path of humanity and the riddle of existence. The sphinx itself unites the four elements, represented through its four-fold spirit.

ASHANTI MANDALA

This is a traditional symbol of the Ashanti people of Ghana. The two-headed crocodile in the middle represents one-ness in plurality, while the crocodile itself is regarded as immortal. The mandala rests on a sacred chair, which stands for earth's divine energy. In the middle of the stylized faces is the sign of the highest, all-encompassing God.

9

AFRICAN MANDALA

Here is another symbol from Ghana. The motif in the middle represents the unity of things. The masks depict the four elements through stylized animal representations. Each section illustrates the different environments that create Unity.

11

African Scorpion Mandala

This two-headed scorpion stands for justice and judgment, since at least two points of view are necessary in order to make a just decision. The scorpion is one of the oldest and most successful animals on the earth. The two birds, which are trying to catch their falling eggs, symbolize the possibility to change all of life's situations.

THE MAZE

The maze illustrates restlessness that one feels in the eternal search of the center, the mystical origin.

THE PRIMEVAL VORTEX

It is represented by two intertwined fish, which reflect the feminine (yin) and masculine (yang) principles.

LEMURESQUE MANDALA

In the middle of the mandalas is the coat of arms—a cross and an eight-pointed star—of the motherland Mu. It is surrounded by sixteen different crosses, which all embody the "Great Four" and which are all directly connected to Mu. These signs were found on stone tablets in Mexico.

SUMERIAN MANDALA

This is a symbolic representation of
the Sumerian god Ea, the god of the
waters. He was portrayed as either half
goat and fish or, as here, as goat and
water, which expresses the fertility of
earth and water.

ARABIC EYE MANDALA

The inner circle stands for divine wisdom and the outer oval represents the feminine principle. The eye projects the outer world to the inside world and vice-versa.

CHINESE DRAGON
MANDALA

The dragon, symbol of life's
eternal turbulence, is on
the hunt for the Luck Pearl,
symbol of perfection, infinity,
and purity.

Assyrian Winged Circle

Between 3,000 B.C.E and 1,000 B.C.E and spanning from Egypt to Mesopotamia, the winged circle was a symbol used in secret Assyrian folk-lore. The wings represent primal forces and the powerful protection that they offer. Wings would later serve as a symbol for archangels.

Egyptian Astronomic Mandala

The star world is in the middle followed by the god world, the human world, and finally the material world—depicted by papyrus and crops. All four worlds influence and depend on one another.

Aztec Mandala

Beginning from the top middle and moving clockwise, this Aztec sun shield uses the following animals to narrate the days and signs of the week: crocodile, wind, house, lizard, snake, skull, stag, rabbit, water, dog, monkey, grass, reed, ocelot, eagle, vulture, motion, flint, knife, rain, flower.

FAIRY MANDALA

These fairies are celebrating
The Dance of Autumn.

CELTIC MANDALA

Manifold representations of spirals are typical in Celtic symbols. This mandala depicts the flow of physical and spiritual energies.

CELTIC CROSS

The Celtic cross is many centuries older than the Christian cross, and it links the circle (feminine energy) to the cross (masculine energy). In the center is the unending knot, a sign of eternity.

CELTIC PROTECTION MANDALA

This mandala was engraved on a shield to protect its owner. The small, innermost square corresponds to the unconscious; the four outer squares are the human spirit, which refer to the physical world. The circles represent different forms of physical and spiritual energies.

Four energy vortices unite into one
cosmic triangle.

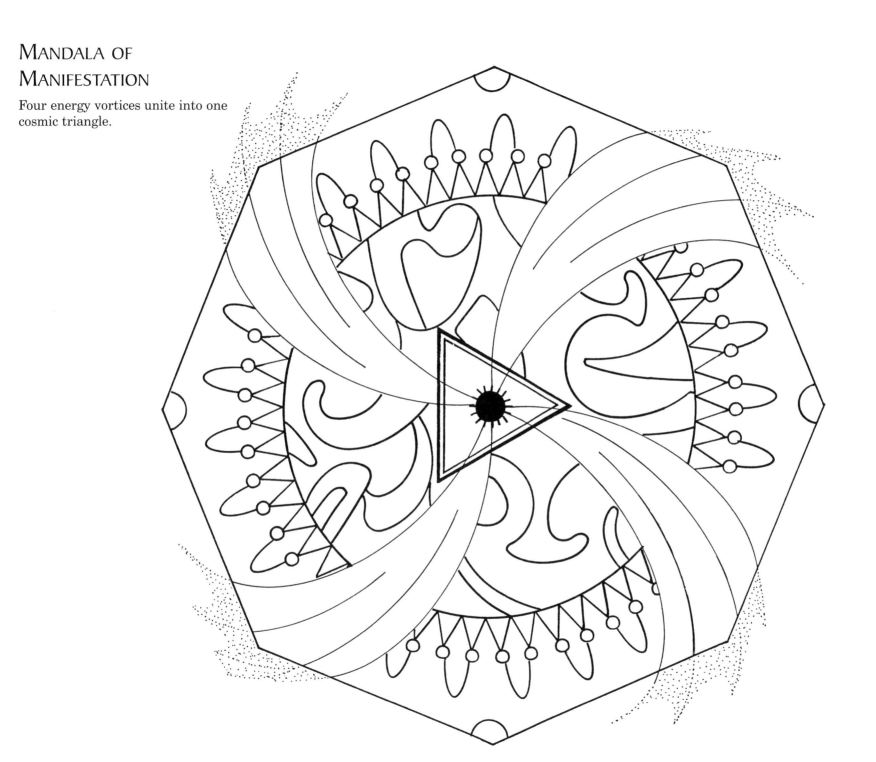

ORNAMENTAL CELTIC MANDALA

The Celtics were fond of ornate decorations, as this mandala clearly shows. In the middle lies a spiral, which symbolizes the origin of creative energy.

PERSIAN MANDALA

This elaborate composition is a typical
example of the Persian carpet weaving.

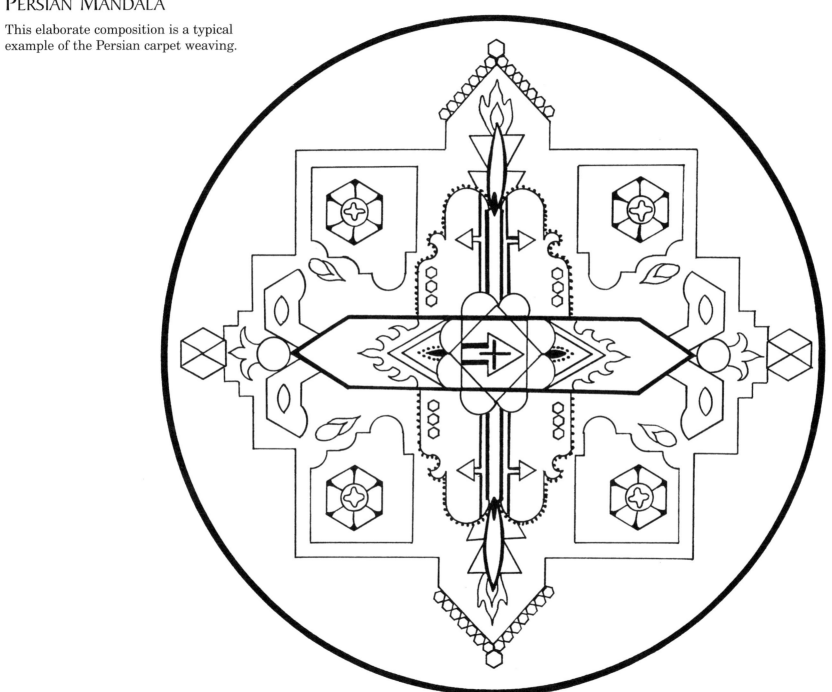

MEDIEVAL MANDORLA

Mandorla means "almond" in Italian. Here, the mandorla encircles the entire saint. The four Evangelists are portrayed on the sides.

ASTROLOGICAL ZODIAC

In the middle of this mandala lies man as Unity, the microcosm in the universe. The written symbols of each astrological sign are in the first circle while the zodiac signs are in the outer circle.

THE ROSE CROSS

This is a holy symbol in secret folklore of the Order of the Rose Cross. It describes how spiritual power develops in us. The Hebraic letters JHWH, which spells God, are inscribed in the cross.

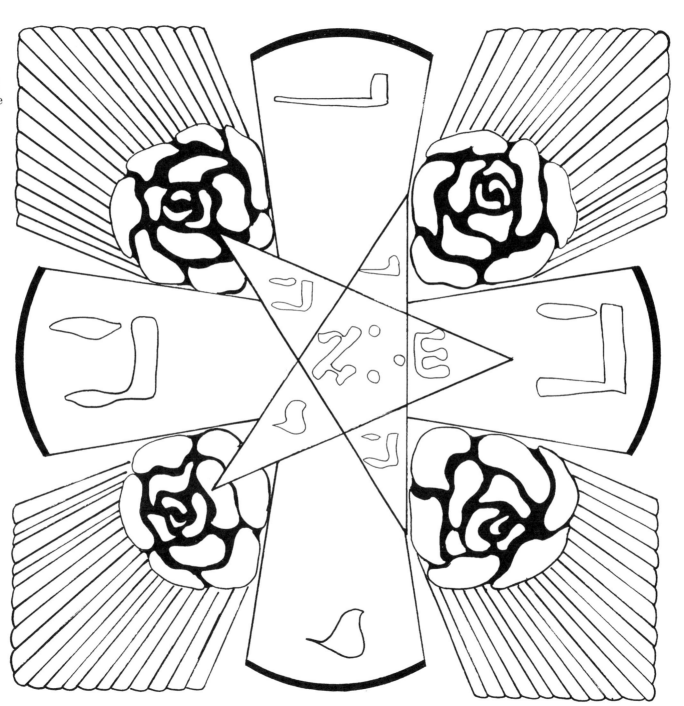

NORWEGIAN MANDALA

This mandala is made of stylized ice
crystals and flowers, which are traditional Norwegian symbols.

CREATION MANDALA

Here the relationship between humans
and the universe is portrayed. In the
outer circle, the Urboros stands as a
symbol for the eternal Cycle of Being.

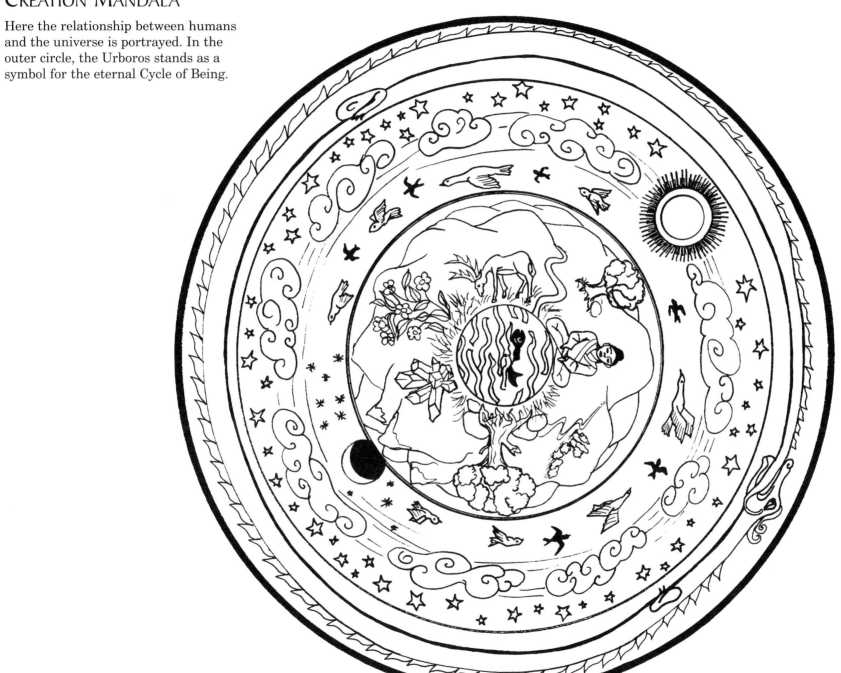

THE DRAGON'S WORLD

The dragon, representing the unity of all good and natural forces, rouses the earth to life by combining the spiritual and the material.

WATER MANDALA

This mandala symbolizes the different water energies that exist.

PRIMAL SHELLFISH

These amoebae with shells can be
found in moorlands and peat lands.

FIRE MANDALA

The triangle embodies the fire principle. The sun is a representation for the planets, a peacock for animals, a diamond for stones, a lion for the zodiac signs, and a rose for plants.

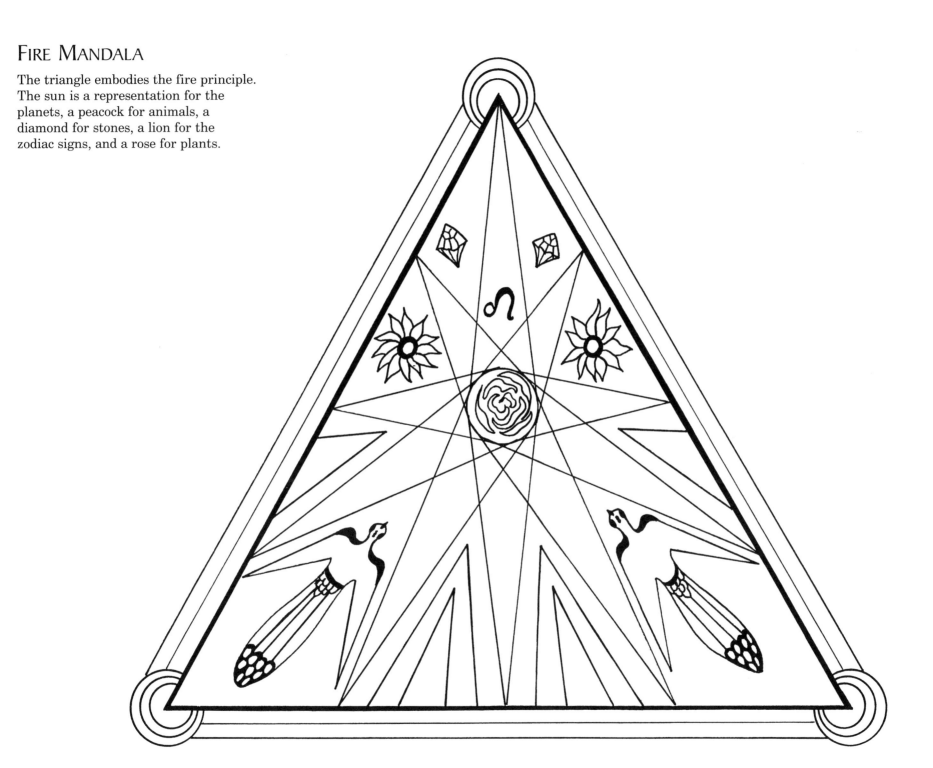

POINTED HOLLOW STAR
MANDALA

Algae, which spreads rapidly in stagnant
water, is made up of several cells within
a symmetrical colony.

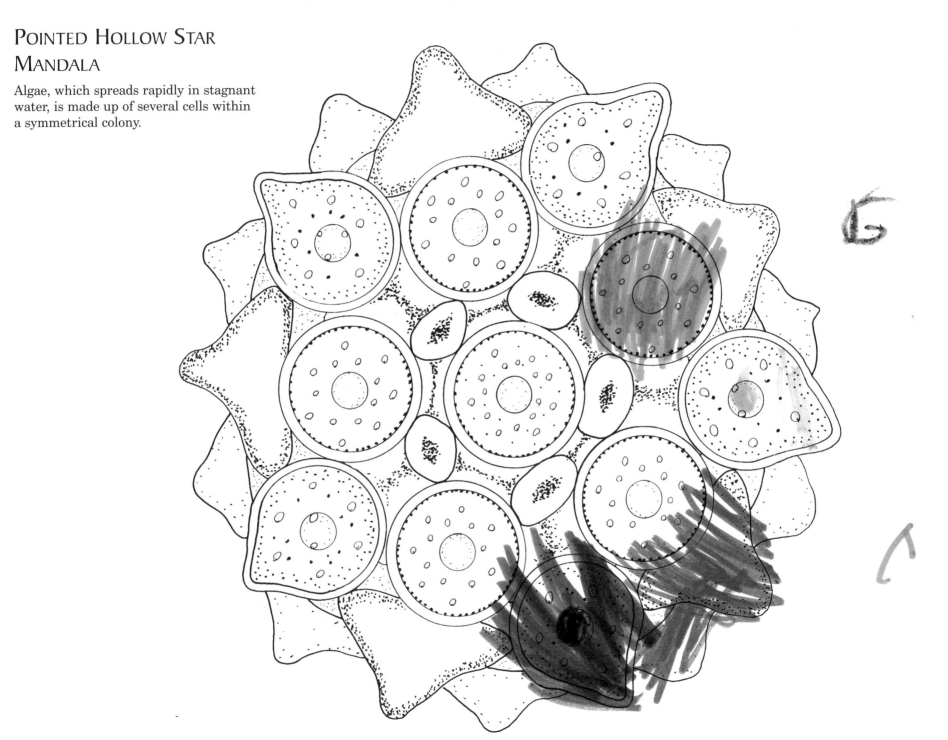

Here, four hummingbirds a[r]
into one stylized blossom.

INUIT MANDALA

The Naskapi Native American tribe usually depicts their highest god as a mandala.

WEB MANDALA

The main lines come from the center, radiate outward, and create—together with diagonal lines—geometric patterns, such as triangles, rhombi, and squares, which in turn create star patterns.

ENERGY MANDALA

In this mandala the four columns in the outer circle represent Heaven while the inner circle describes the progression of life from its cosmic center. The lightning symbolizes heavenly life-giving energy.

"Om Mani Padme Hum" (Praised Be the Crystal in the Lotus)

The inner circle stands for inspiration. In the Lotus flower's petals are the written Tibetan symbols of the mantra.

THE DANCING GOD SHIVA

Shiva, one of the three main gods in Hinduism, is seen as the destroyer and renewer in nature. Through his whirling, cosmic dance, he moves the world. He dances upon the back of the Forgetfulness and Inattentiveness demon. A ring of fire and light surrounds him.

INDIAN MANDALA

This Indian mandala represents the different cosmic spheres.

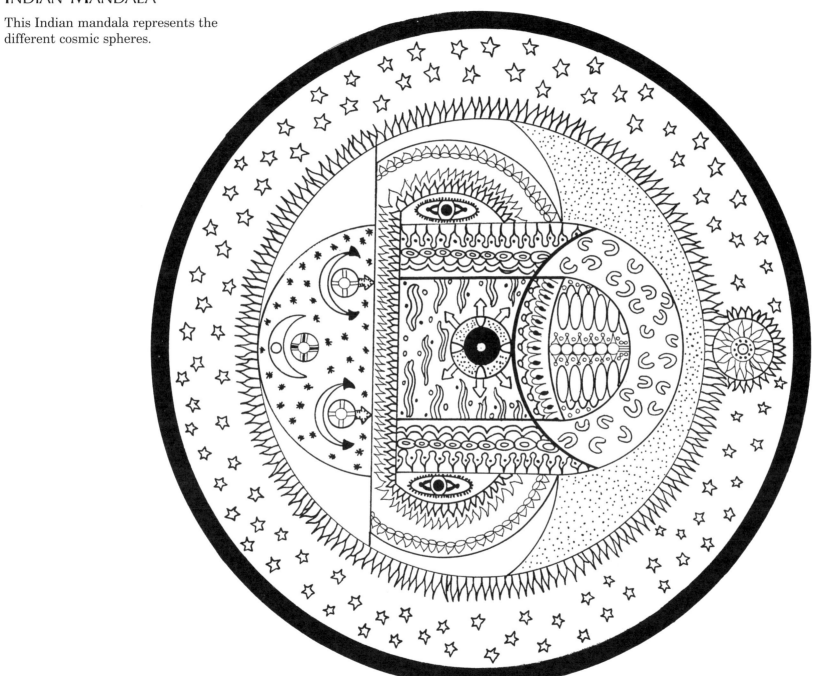

THE SIDDHA CHAKRA

This religious diagram is from the
Dschainas from Rajashtan, India. It is
portrayed by a Lotus flower with eight
petals and describes the way to the
highest stage of Being.

THE BUDDHIST FISH

The Shining Eye of the Spirit is in this
Buddhist fish. The spirit is trying to
move upward to the Inner and the Outer.

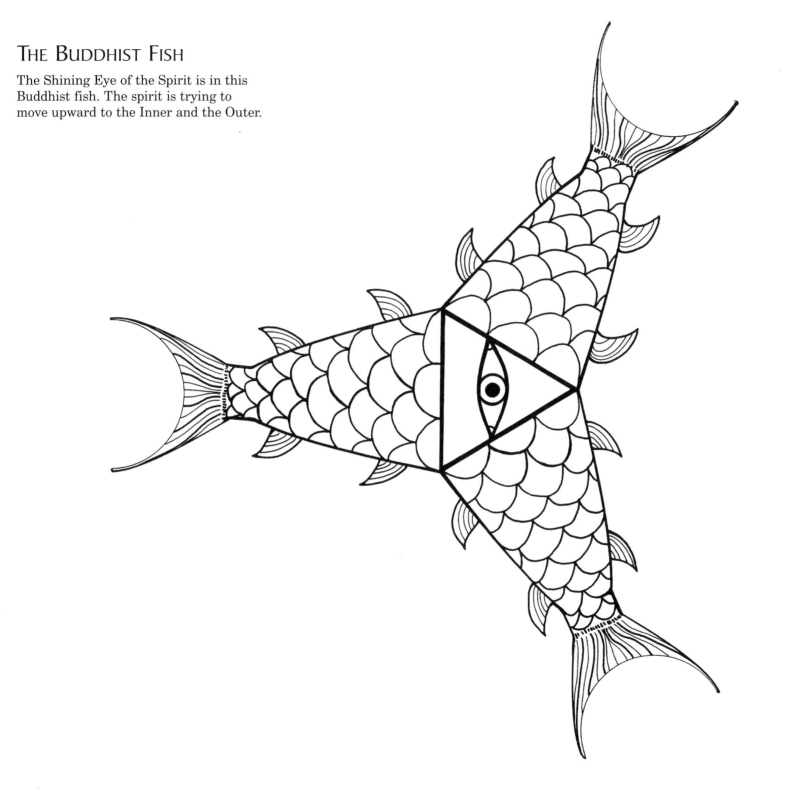

TREE MANDALA

The roots of the trees, along with
their spirits, are united in the center.

Rose Mandala

The rose is a symbol of light, love, and
life. The fairies are dancing among the
petals, inviting you to come and enjoy
the rose's invigorating fragrance.

The Aboriginal Rainbow Snake

The twin Rainbow Snake encompasses the collective and creative power of menstruating women, which can be both destructive and healing.

DREAM MANDALA

This Aboriginal mandala uses insects
and lizards to represent earth's energy.

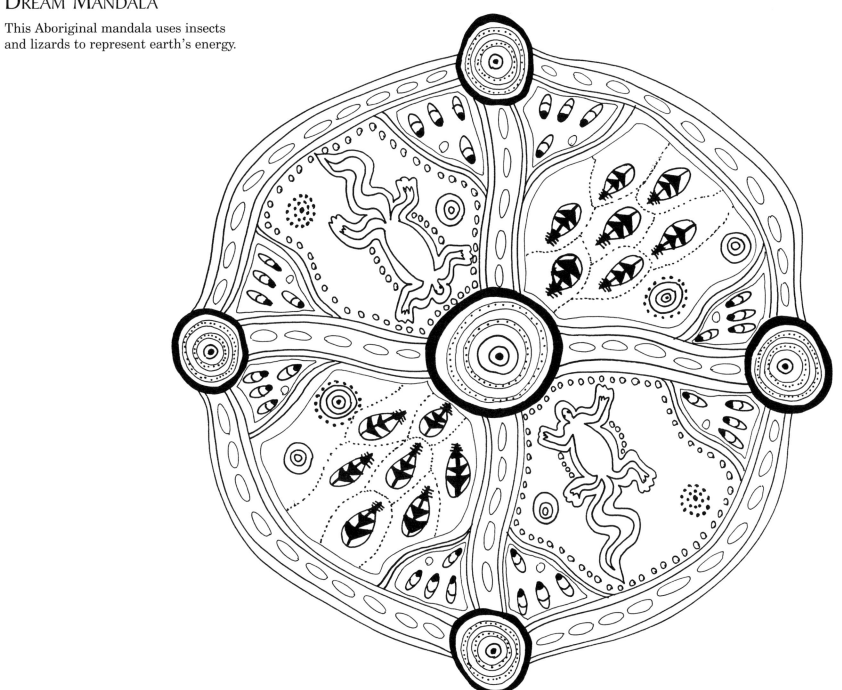

ABORIGINAL EARTH MANDALA

Earth's different energy fields, illustrated by circles and waves, surround the snake, which represents feminine power.

CIRCLE MANDALA

Circles intertwine with another to
reflect atomic structur

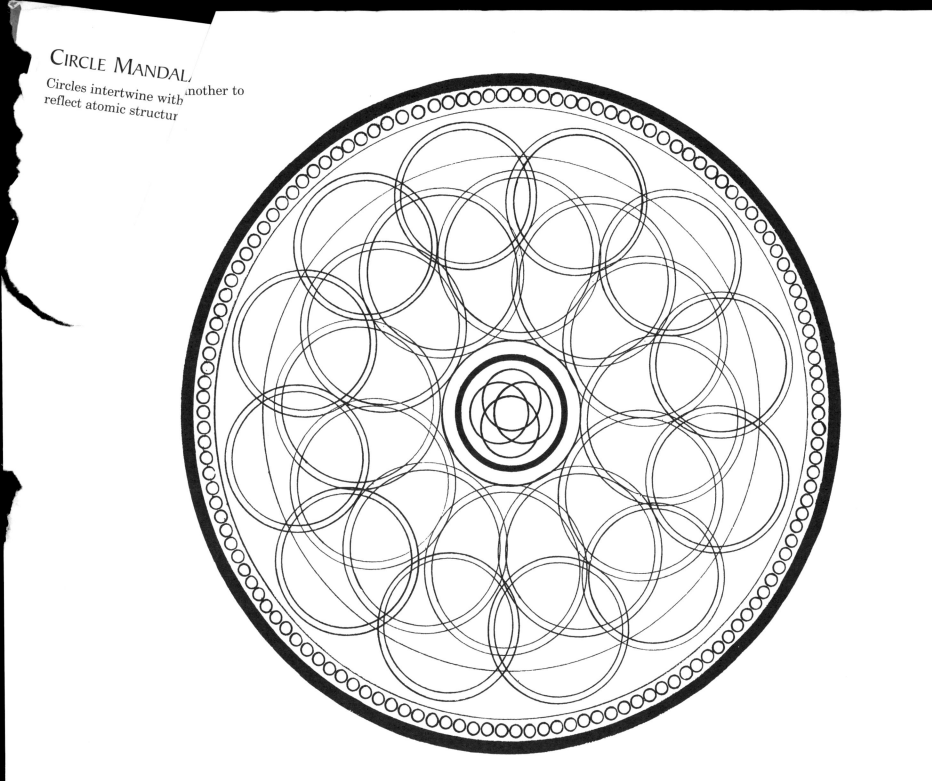

COSMIC MANDALA

FL

The cosmic mandala is shape[...]even
spheres and their intersectio[...] A [...]
nu

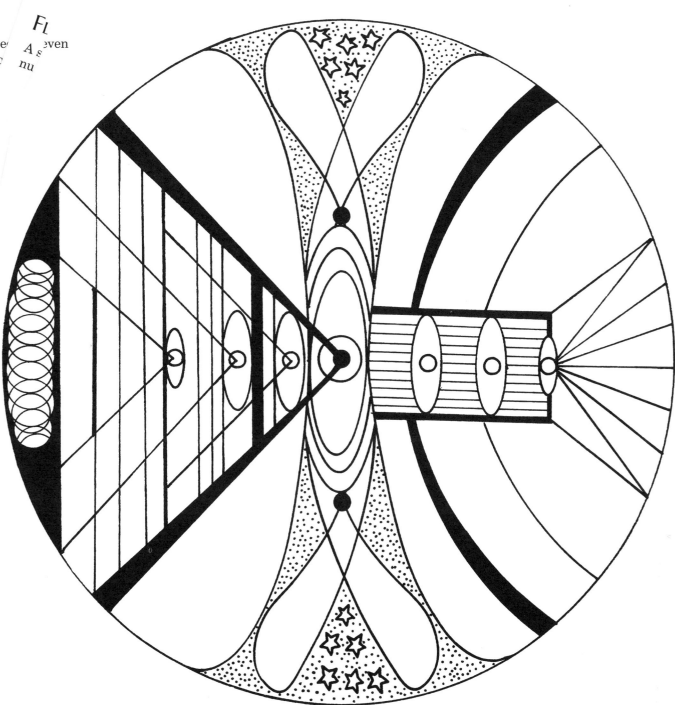

THE SEAL OF SOLOMON

The Star of David is in the middle of this mandala. The upward triangle stands for fire and masculine energy; the downward triangle represents water and feminine energy. The outer border describes the alliance between God and man.

Rosette Mandala

This mandala is derived from the window rosettes in sacred Christian art.

SPIDER WEB

The spider web was regarded by the
Celts as the fabric that holds the world
together.

SEA ANEMONE

NATIVE AMERICAN MANDALA

The sun and moon's powers are combined and surrounded by the eternally renewing snake in the middle of this Native American mandala. In the outer circle the four elements take on the following animal forms: the eagle is air and the Elevated; the dolphin is water and Intelligence; the tortoise is earth and Patience; and the horse is fire and Power.

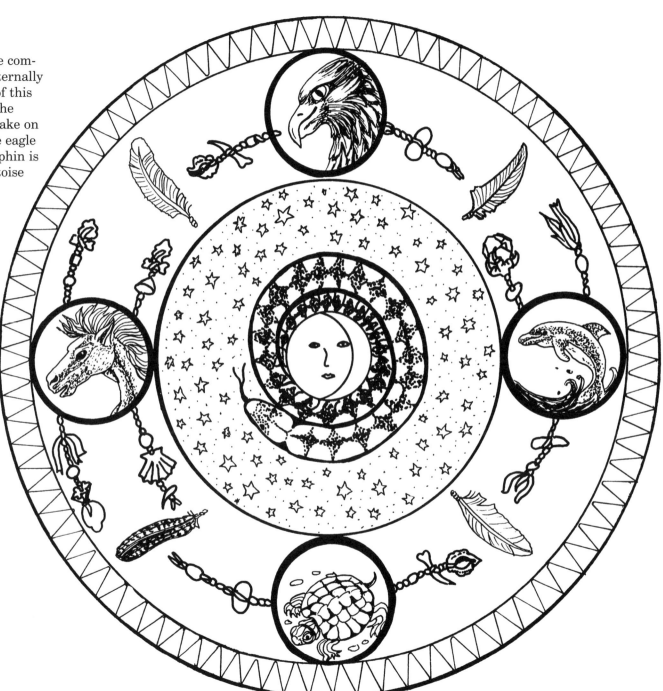

NAVAHO MANDALA

This classic Navaho sand
painting describes the order
of the world.

HOPI MANDALA

Beginning in the upper left and continuing
clockwise, the Hopi mandala tells the
history of The Snake Legend.

NATIVE AMERICAN
SHAMANISTIC MANDALA

This mandala describes the relationship
between humans and nature.

NATIVE AMERICAN MEDICINE WHEEL

The magical medicine wheel in Native American culture was used for protection and healing.

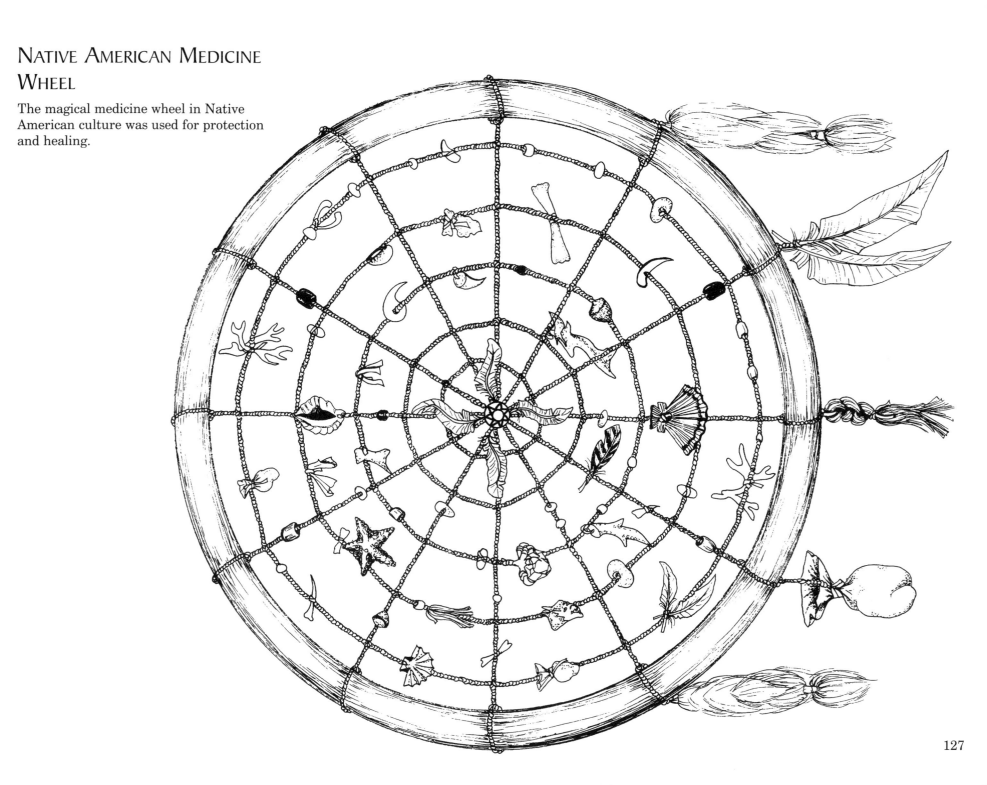

NATIVE AMERICAN MANDALA

The four elements—embodied through
animals—are integrating with humans,
represented by the handprints. The sun
and moon influence all life.

ICE CRYSTAL MANDALA

Each ice crystal is unique, yet all have one
thing in common: six sides.

HUMMINGBIRDS

Join the hummingbirds as they smell
the flower mandala.

EVOLUTION MANDALA

The Lotus was the first flower on earth. From inside to outside, this represents the progression of life through concentric circles.

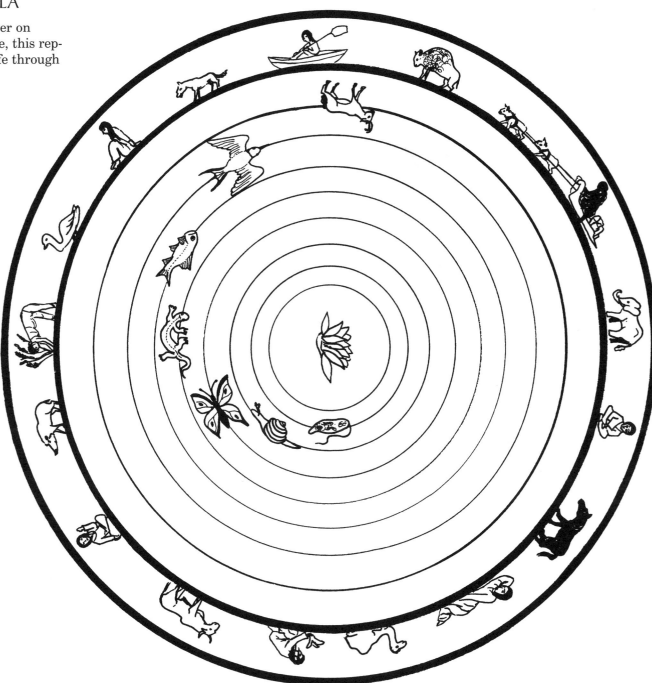

135

MANDALA OF THE FOUR ELEMENTS

This represents the four elements and their respective manifestations, symbolized by the stupas. The square is earth, the circle is water, the triangle is fire, and the half-circle is air.

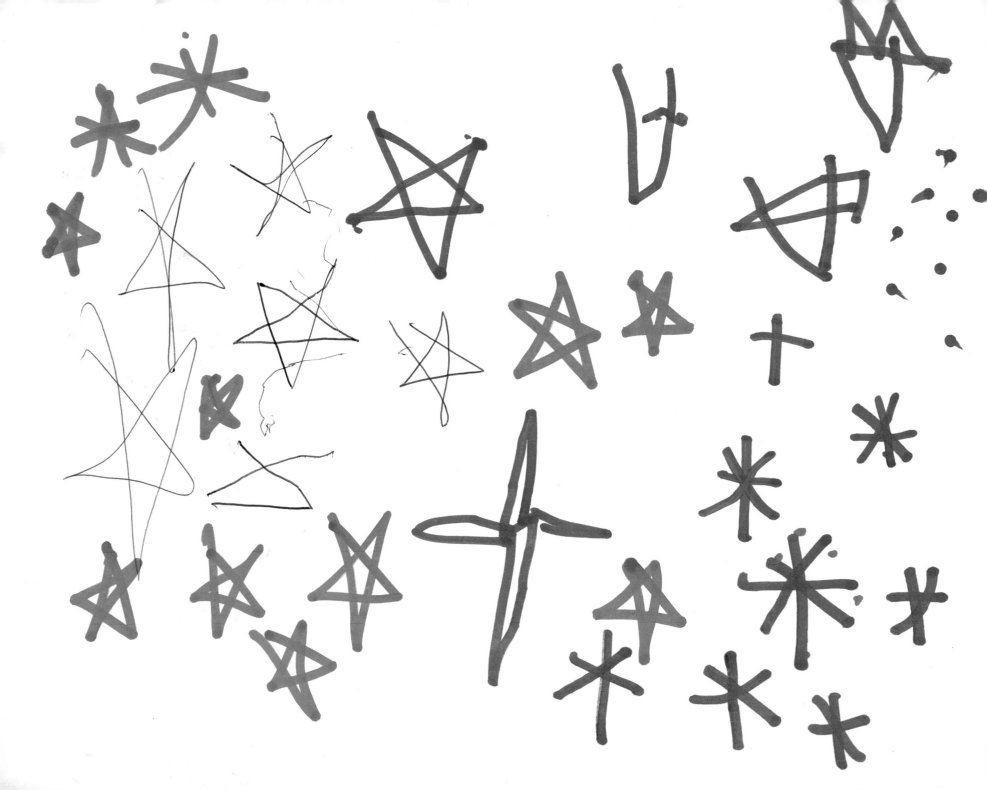

POLYNESIAN SHIELD MANDALA

This typical Polynesian protection mandala was placed on a warrior's shield.

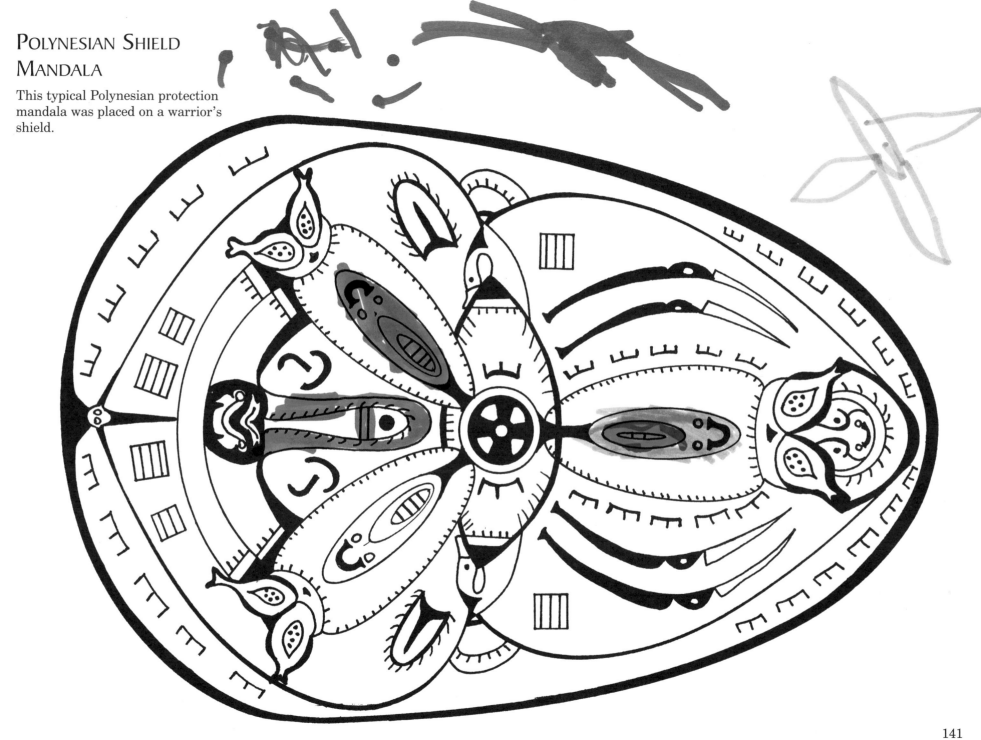

POLYNESIAN MANDALA

Here is another powerful Polynesian symbol of a face with intertwined birds and fishes.

FIRE DRAGON

This fire dragon stands for the
tremendous power of Creation.

MANDALA OF LIFE

Human consciousness rises from the
unconscious of plants and crystals.

WHAT COLORS REPRESENT

Interpreting the colors you use to color your mandalas is an important step in your journey to self-discovery and self-healing. They can help you to find, recognize, and release those hidden and trapped feelings, emotions, and fears, enabling you to express yourself clearly. While we color, we are subconsciously picking specific colors which represent what we are feeling at the moment. Below you will find what some basic colors may reveal about yourself. Only look at this list after you have finished coloring *all* of the mandalas in this book. Do not be alarmed if you have some negative representations. They are not judgments but rather simply demonstrate how a color can affect you.

YELLOW: Positive: sun, light, brightness, joy, contentment, inspiration, development, liberation, wisdom, intellect, imagination, enthusiasm, free spirit. Negative: fear of enclosure, superficial, envious, overestimation of self.

ORANGE: Positive: optimism, energy, zest for life, ambition, joy, activity, tenderness, open-minded, courage, strength, warmth, youthfulness, health, self-confidence. Negative: hatred, impulsiveness, rage.

PINK: Positive: romance, affection, devotion, softness, unselfishness, feminine, restraint, tenderness, pleasurable, elegant, willpower. Negative: inhibited, defenseless, sentimental, lack of reality.

PURPLE: Positive: super-ego, meditative, spirituality, mystic, magic, inspiration, unity of contrasts, sensitivity, individualism. Negative: sorrow, melancholy, privation, renunciation, aversion.

BLUE: Positive: security, balance, calm, peace, quiet, tranquility, relaxation, freedom, limitless, longing, loyalty, idealism, unselfishness, reason. Negative: emptiness, boredom, paralysis, naïveté.

TURQUOISE: Positive: friendship, sociability, communication, innovative, self-confidence, grace, charm, humor. Negative: capricious, self-centered, need for recognition.

GREEN: Positive: life, nature, hope, willpower, constancy, balance, growth, new beginnings, recovery, well-being, integrity, perceptive, tenacity, determination. Negative: ambitious, dishonesty, drive for power.

BLACK/GRAY: Positive: revival, renewal, dignity, unconquerable. Negative: death, destruction, mourning, lack of movement, sin, fear, loss, threatening, darkness, loneliness, hopelessness, compulsive, aversion.

WHITE: Positive: purity, innocence, perfection, virtue, objectivity, sublimity, redemption, reliability, sincerity, love of truth, business instinct. Negative: coldness, perfectionist.

Index

Aborginal Rainbow Snake, 99

Aboriginal Earth Mandala, 103

African Mandala, 11

African Scorpion Mandala, 13

Arabic Eye Mandala, 25

Ashanti Mandala, 9

Assyrian Winged Circle, 29

Astrological Zodiac, 51

Aztec Mandala, 33

Buddhist Fish, 93

Celtic Mandala, 37

Celtic Mandala, 39

Celtic Protection Mandala, 41

Chinese Dragon Mandala, 27

Circle Mandala, 105

Cosmic Mandala, 109

Creation Mandala, 57

Dancing God Shiva, 87

Dragon's World, 59

Dream Mandala, 101

Dynamic Whale Mandala, 75

Egyptian Astronomic Mandala, 31

Energy Mandala, 83

Evolution Mandala, 135

Fairy Mandala, 35

Fire Dragon, 145

Fire Mandala, 67

Flower Mandala with Turkish Decoration, 61

Flower Mandala, 107

Heike Owusu, 1

Hopi Mandala, 123

Hummingbirds, 133

Ice Crystal Mandala, 131

Indian Mandala, 89

Introduction, 1

Inuit Mandala, 77

Lemuresque Mandala, 19

Magical Energy Mandala, 3

Mandala of Life, 147

Mandala of Manifestation, 43

Mandala of the Flower Fairies, 149

Mandala of the Four Elements, 137

Maze, 15

Medieval Mandorla, 49

Mediterranean Mandala, 23

Native American Mandala, 119

Native American Mandala, 129

Native American Medicine Wheel, 127

Native American Shamanistic Mandala, 125

Navaho Mandala, 121

Norwegian Mandala, 55

"Om Mani Padme Hum," 85

Ornamental Celtic Mandala, 45

Peacock Mandala, 5

Persian Mandala, 47

Pointed Hollow Star Mandala, 69

Polynesian Mandala, 143

Polynesian Shield Mandala, 141

Primal Shellfish, 65

Primeval Vortex, 17

Rose Cross, 53

Rose Mandala, 97

Rosette Mandala, 113

Rosette-Shaped Mandala, 79

Sea Anemone, 117

Seal of Solomon, 111

Siddha Chakra, 91

Sphinx Mandala, 7

Spider Web, 115

Spring Mandala, 71

Sumerian Mandala, 21

Sun Face, 139

Tree Mandala, 95

Unity, 73

Water Mandala, 63

Web Mandala, 81

What Colors Represent, 151